5 2
Little Parables
from Ireland

A one-year weekly devotional
with inspirational writings,
scripture verses and prayers

Sally Ireland Kennedy

CREATION
HOUSE
PRESS

52 LITTLE PARABLES FROM IRELAND by Sally I. Kennedy
Published by Creation House Press
A part of Strang Communications Company
600 Rinehart Road
Lake Mary, Florida 32746
www.creationhouse.com

All Scripture references, unless otherwise indicated, are from are from the Holy Bible, New International Version. Copyright © 1973, 1978, 1984, International Bible Society. Used by permission.

Cover and interior design by Debbie Lewis

Library of Congress Catalog Card Number: 2002103145
International Standard Book Number: 0-88419-892-8

02 03 04 05   87654321
Printed in the United States of America

To Contact the Author:

Sally I. Kennedy
P.O. Box 1648
Boca Raton, FL 33429
Phone: (561) 912-9906
Fax: (561) 912-9306
Email: SallyIKennedy@aol.com

For Ben

ACKNOWLEDGEMENTS

I would like to thank first of all my husband. I love you, Ben.

Thank you to my precious grandchildren Taylor, McCallen and Jackson Kennedy, Ryan and Tommy Haag and Courtney, Benjamin and Michael Kennedy, who let me be a kid with them. To their moms and dads, Lisa and Todd, Adrienne and David and Teri and Benjie, thank you! I love you.

Thank you to my sister and best critic, Marion Smith. Thanks to my reunion group—Bev Abt, Mary Jasco, Jeanne Scott and Joy Thibodeau—for all their support. Thank you to my balcony friend Cathy Coney, to Justin Steurer for spiritual direction, and to Cathy Karpinen for her kindness and prayers. Thank you to Warren Kramer at Gospel Com., who first posted my writings, and to Jim Croft, who encouraged me to publish.

Most of all, thanks to my truest friend, Jesus, for being with me through this whole adventure, to my wonderful heavenly Father who so kindly allows me to see the "moments," and to the Holy Spirit who gives me inspiration—and perseverance—to write.

TABLE OF CONTENTS

FOREWORD

There are a myriad of tiny moments in our lives when God breaks through and reveals His presence to us, sometimes with a whisper, sometimes with a shout.

This collection of inspirational writings comes from some of these times in my life during the last couple of years.

Be blessed as you read, and as you become continually more aware of His reality in the ordinary—every day.

—*SALLY IRELAND KENNEDY*

I will pour out my Spirit on all people.

Your sons and daughters will prophesy,

your old men will dream dreams,

your young men will see visions.

JOEL 2:28

WEEK I

BEATS COUNTING SHEEP

About midnight on Saturday, October 6, I dreamed that as dawn was just beginning here, across the world in Afghanistan it was just starting to get dark. In my dream the United States was starting to bomb Afghanistan. It was dark and fuzzy, with bright lights streaking the sky from time to time, and it resembled the live TV images from Desert Storm.

I woke up and could not go back to sleep until about 4 A.M., which is weird because I sleep like a rock. While I was awake, I prayed for each of my family members by name. When I ran out of things to think and pray about, I asked God if maybe I was awake for some reason. Did He want me to be praying about something? I didn't get any answer, so I just prayed for our country, for wisdom for the President and our leaders, and for protection for them and their families and so on.

The next day around noon I saw on television that we had started bombing Afghanistan. It was just getting dark there, and the live pictures looked like what I had seen in my dream. I believe God did wake me in the night to have me intercede in prayer for our nation.

When you can't get to sleep at night, maybe it is for a higher purpose. Just ask the Lord to show you if there is something—or somebody—that needs prayer, and you will be blessed to intercede. It beats counting sheep!

PRAYER: Father, when I am tossing and turning at night, and sleep is just not coming, set off a little bell in my brain to remind me to use this time to talk to You, and to lift up people and situations that You bring to my mind and heart. Thank You, Lord, for this privilege. In Jesus' name, amen.

But the Lord is faithful,

and he will strengthen and protect you

from the evil one.

2 THESSALONIANS 3:3

WEEK 2

BYE BYE BULLY

Three doves were scurrying around on the wooden deck outside my study window. Doves are ground feeders, and this morning they were vying for the seeds tossed out of the feeder by other birds.

I never knew that doves—or birds—are territorial, but apparently they are. One continued to bully the other two. The "pecking" order worked, and the two backed off.

While the bully enjoyed the pickings that remained, a large brown sea grape leaf blew across the deck. About 5 or 6 inches across, it tumbled right up behind the bully. That startled the bird, who then left the place he had claimed for his own.

There's an enemy who tries to bully me. At times Satan attempts to intimidate me while he stakes a momentary or temporary claim in a situation. A chicken is the kind of bird that he is. But Satan will quickly retreat when frightened by the presence of the King.

It is reassuring to remember that whenever I am bothered and hassled with doubts and fears from the enemy, I can resist him in Jesus' name, and he will flee (James 4:7). That's good news!

PRAYER: Father, please help me remember today that, in the war with Satan, the battlefield is my mind. I pray the blood of Jesus over my mind, and put on all of the armor of God (Eph. 6). Then I will stand and know that the battle ultimately belongs to the Lord. Thank You, Lord! Amen.

God did not give us a spirit of timidity,

but a spirit of power, of love

and of self-discipline.

2 TIMOTHY 1:7

WEEK 3

CLEANING

During a holiday weekend, I took a walk to a church in our neighborhood. There had been several holiday services, with more to come; many people were in and out of the place in just a few days.

Yet there was order. Everything was clean and neat and straightened up. One man was quietly and methodically going about cleaning the pews, straightening books and discarding old bulletins. Here was this gentleman, cleaning God's house in a calm, disciplined manner.

Am I not called to do the same with me—God's "temple" or house?

PRAYER: Father, I praise You that Jesus lives in my heart and that the Holy Spirit dwells in me. Please help me to regularly weed out, clean out and straighten out my life. In Jesus' name, amen.

Do not be anxious about anything,

but in everything, by prayer and petition, with

thanksgiving, present your requests to God.

PHILIPPIANS 4:6

WEEK 4

CLOSED UP AND SHUT DOWN

Big, full anemone-type flowers in bright lemon yellows and neon pinks cluster about our front walkway. They really catch the eye, and they thrive in the brutal heat of our tropical days.

At night, however, they close up and shut down. The droopy gray-green succulent leaves look nearly dead. In fact, you probably wouldn't even notice them at all.

Have you heard the saying, "Pray at night and give your problems to the Lord; He'll be up all night anyway"?

It is so comforting to know that God is never closed up and shut down; "He who watches over you will not slumber," (Ps. 121:3).

That is good news!

PRAYER: Father, it is so good to know that You always hear me, no matter what time, what day or what the circumstance may be. And thank You, Father, that while I am even just coming to You, You are already answering. Amen!

I have hidden your word in my heart

that I might not sin against you.

PSALM 119:11

WEEK 5

CRACKS

While walking in my neighborhood, I noticed that some of the older sidewalk sections have interesting plants growing up through the cracks. Some appear to be scraggly weeds, while others look like colorful and pretty flowers.

How very quickly nature reverts to the wild when ungroomed—just as the grass in the sidewalk does. When we have cracks and openings and holes to which we don't pay attention, how quickly all sorts of things materialize and take root there.

Daily, or at least regularly, I must take care to tend to those areas, or the "old nature" will take over and it will be "as before."

PRAYER: Lord, please help me to take the time I need to talk with You, to read Your Word, to listen to Your music, to be with other Christians. Thank You for all the ways You provide for me to be fed and to grow in my new nature. In Jesus' name, amen.

You will go out in joy and be led forth in peace;

the mountains and hills will burst into

song before you, and all the trees of the field

will clap their hands.

ISAIAH 55:12

WEEK 6

DANCING ON THE MOUNTAIN

The trees of the field will clap their hands," says the song from Psalms. I like that song but have always thought the words were sort of stupid—until that day on the top of the mountain. Sitting on a grassy plateau overlooking valleys, mountain peaks and somewhere down there rivers and towns, I beheld an alpine meadow strewn with wildflowers and blanketed with patches of purple lupine, yellow and orange paintbrush and ivory milkweed. I understood.

As at the Sermon on the Mount, we too were sitting around listening to a man teach. That's when I noticed that the tall grass was dancing and waving in the breeze and that the swaying branches of the blue spruce were "clapping" as they moved.

Fr. Michael waved his arm widely, and said, "If God can do all this [panorama] with dirt, think of what He can do with us."

Yes, think!

PRAYER: Lord, thank You for making me "beautiful," that others might see Your beauty in me and be drawn to You. In Jesus' name, amen.

If any of you lacks wisdom, he should ask God,

who gives generously to all without finding fault,

and it will be given to him.

JAMES 1:5

WEEK 7

DECISION AND DIRECTION

While out for a morning walk today, I turned a corner and saw a white cowbird, similar to a small heron, right in the middle of where two streets came together. He was quietly standing still, as if trying to decide which way to go. He wasn't ruffled by my appearance and nearly let me walk right up to him. He was in his own world for the moment.

How often I stand at the crossroads of a decision. If I would come out of my own world of thoughts and look to the Lord for direction, things would go so much smoother.

Thank You, Father, that You always have a direction for us to follow and that you always are so willing to reveal it to us when we ask.

PRAYER: Lord, I praise You that You really do order the steps of a righteous person. Thank You that I am righteous in Your eyes because of the shed blood of Jesus. Glory to You, O Lord. Amen!

Let us run with perseverance the race

marked out for us. Let us fix our eyes on Jesus,

the author and perfecter of our faith.

HEBREWS 12:1–2

Week 8

Determined

It was a hot, cloudless autumn morning. As I was waking up and enjoying a cup of coffee, my attention was drawn to the bird feeder hanging outside of my study. The feeder is a Plexiglas tube with a small rimmed saucer underneath, and it is squirrel-proof—supposedly.

Sitting in the saucer, though, was the most contented squirrel, munching away to his heart's content on the delicious sunflower seeds meant especially for cardinals.

The determined squirrel had overcome some obstacles to get from his nest high in the palm fronds to the bird feeder. Once he'd gotten there, it was no doubt difficult to climb onto the slippery feeding tray. He'd calculated his timing so there were no birds at the feeder; he could have it all to himself without a fight.

He persevered. He was determined. He got his nourishment because he purposed to do so. Today I must decide and purpose to get the spiritual food I desire—and need—to both stay alive and to grow in my faith.

PRAYER: Lord, thank You for the path You have carefully carved out for me in this life. Lord, You know that I get tired sometimes and I need Your gift of perseverance. Please help me to hang in there. In Jesus' name, amen.

Taste and see that the LORD is good;

blessed is the man who takes refuge in him.

PSALM 34:8

WEEK 9

DOTS AND DROPS

Those pesky ants were back again, this time in the bathroom. They kept a steady stream going back and forth from the sink to behind the light switch, keeping in close touch with one another to stay on the right path. They were coming to get little drinks of water, bits of toothpaste or maybe soap.

I put a tiny dot of syrupy ant poison near the switch. Then I put a huge drop of it on a cardboard square near the sink. Slowly the ants began to gather on the smaller dot. They ignored the bigger drop, passing right by it to get to where the other ants were gathering.

Eventually the ants would take the chemical back to the colony, and that would be the end of my ant problem for the time being. Considering the ants' behavior, these questions occurred to me: How often do I pass up a banquet just because others are going for the morsel? And, will just one tiny little bit of poison eventually kill me?

We are in a day-to-day combat zone. There is a war going on in the heavenlies between the forces of good and evil. Our minds are the frontline of the battleground. We can choose not to join others who are hanging around the poisonous dots that are everywhere in the world. Little things can build up and add up and can make us spiritually very sick.

Each day God presents us with a beautiful array: nature, His Word, His kindness and new mercies, His loving companionship, protection and unlimited grace. We can "eat" His "food" until we are stuffed and never wonder if, because it is so palatable, it could be bad for us.

PRAYER: Help me, O God, to choose You every day; to make You my portion today and every day. In Jesus' name, amen.

In his heart a man plans his course,

but the LORD *determines his steps.*

PROVERBS 16:9

WEEK 10

EASY WAY OUT

Have you ever been in a swimming pool and tried to swim against the flow of the water jets, or been in the ocean and tried to swim against the current?

It is a lot of work just to stay in one place. It is even more work to go against the flow. On the other hand, have you noticed how effortless it is just to relax and let the current carry you along?

In our spiritual swimming, it is more difficult to move along when we are going on our own steam—uphill, against the flow, doing things our own way. We can get a lot farther, a lot quicker, with a lot less effort, by going in the direction the Lord has planned for us.

Today I would like to remember to take the easy way out—let God be in charge, and go with the flow.

PRAYER: Today, Lord, please help me to relax and sit back in the boat, and let You be the one up front paddling. Thank You, Lord! In Jesus' name, amen.

"For I know the plans I have for you," declares

the LORD, *"plans to prosper you and not to harm*

you, plans to give you hope and a future."

JEREMIAH 29:11

Week 11

Even for Leaves

This has been such a warm, dry autumn. The leaf colors won't peak as they have in other years. That beautiful fall foliage won't arrive in all of its splendor as it has some other years. It *is* coming—just late, and slowly.

The leaves are having a hard time changing. Change is hard for me too. It seems that the older I get, the less I welcome it. The old and familiar are so comfortable. "Letting go and letting God" seems to be the best way—certainly the most painless and probably the most effective, too.

It's a good thing God doesn't tire of growing and changing us. He'll keep doing it as fast as we continue to let Him, and He is never content to leave us where we are. So that means change!

Change is difficult, even for leaves, but it is the perfect plan. And, it's good to remember that wherever we go, God already is there.

That's good news.

PRAYER: Father, change is a sure bet for me. Nothing stays the same, except You. You alone are the same yesterday, today and forever. Help me remember that change is part of Your perfect plan for my life. In Jesus' name, amen.

"No one knows about that day or hour,

not even the angels in heaven, nor the Son,

but only the Father."

MATTHEW 24:36

WEEK 12:

"EVERYTHING'S READY!"

My daughter's voice was brimming with excitement and anticipation as she happily shared with me all the details for the nursery. *"Everything is ready! Now we just need the baby to get here!"*

There was lot of hype about Y2K and lot of talk about the second coming of Christ. There were some wonderful words of wisdom floating about; there also were some frightening scare tactics essentially warning us to get right with God in the short time we had left before Jesus would return.

Through the ages, and still today, events happen in God's time. Everything happens in the fullness of God's time. The Son of God, our Lord Jesus Christ, was born at the precise fullness of God's time, as a baby in Bethlehem two thousand years ago.

Jesus himself said that He didn't know the time of his return, so it is unlikely that we could know. It isn't necessary for us to know. When "everything's ready," Jesus will come again. In the meantime, if we turn our hearts toward Jesus, and focus on our relationship with Him, we have nothing to fear.

We can be with Him now, and we can be with Him forever when He comes again to take us where He is—when everything's ready.

PRAYER: Lord, thank You for the promise that Jesus left—that He is going to return and take me where He is, to be forever in glory with Him. Maranatha! Come quickly, Lord Jesus. Amen.

Anyone who will not receive the kingdom of God

like a little child will never enter it.

MARK 10:15

WEEK 13

EXCITED

My wonderful granddaughter, McCallen, is four-and-a-half years old. Whenever I go to McCallen's house, she tries to get my car keys and then scrambles to get her shoes. She runs to the door and waits right there for me, knowing I can't get to the car without going out the door, and can't leave without the keys.

It doesn't matter what day I visit, or what time, or what is going on—she still is determined that she's going with me when I leave that house. She has no idea where I might take her in the car or what we might do, but that does not diminish her excitement or anticipation about going and being with me.

In my life journey I am often more interested in knowing—or trying to find out—where God is taking me than in being excited about just being with Him.

I go to great lengths to insure McCallen's safety and well being and to provide good things and fun times for her while she is with me. Can I trust my heavenly Father do all of that—and more—for me? Jeremiah 29:11 says, "For I know the plans I have for you," declares the LORD, "plans to prosper you and not to harm you, plans to give you hope and a future."

That is good news.

PRAYER: Lord, thank You that You know where You are taking me, even when I don't have a clue. Thank You that Your plans for me are always good, and that for those who love You, Lord, all things work together for their good. In Jesus' name, amen.

*The L*ORD *will keep you from all harm—*

he will watch over your life;

*the L*ORD *will watch over your coming and going*

both now and forevermore.

PSALM 121:7–8

WEEK 14

FARAWAY PLACE

We were winging our way home, still in the afterglow of a long Spring weekend. How green were the budding trees and rolling hills of middle Tennessee. On the initial landing approach to Atlanta, I found my thoughts of thanksgiving for safe travel being translated into whispered prayers. *Thank You, Father, for a safe trip.* The memory pages began to flip, and I began to see the many trips the Lord has allowed us to take with a safe return—trips all the way around the world to Israel, to Germany and to Africa.

We don't have to leave home to journey to a faraway place. What about the journey into inner-child work, where there is healing upon a safe return? How about the long walk of grief after separation or loss of someone or something? Safe arrival brings comfort and peace. There is that most blessed of all journeys that seems light years away, but is truly a blink away—the journey when you meet Jesus Himself, just you and Him on the road, and the wonder and awe of that safe destination.

To what place are you now journeying? Where do you want to safely arrive?

PRAYER: Thank You, Father, that no matter where my journey in life may take me, You are with me. Thank You for providing angels to assist me on my journey, and for the guidance of the Holy Spirit. In Jesus' name, amen.

The thief comes only to steal and kill

and destroy; I have come that they

may have life, and have it to the full.

John 10:10

WEEK 15

FLUFFY

Traveling to Orlando by commuter plane, we had to fly through some low clouds—those lovely puffy clouds, in varying shades of white to light and medium gray. They all looked so beautiful from inside the airplane—so light, so fluffy, so safe. Yet we experienced mild to medium turbulence while in their vicinity.

Isn't this what happens with destructive forces in our lives? Things can look so good, so harmless; we are lulled into deception by the calm, fluffy, pretty way sin looks. Then when we're into it, we find out the turbulence it causes for us and for those who are traveling with us.

Fortunately, there is a way out; the answer really is *Jesus!*

PRAYER: Thank You, Lord, for providing so many ways to fend off the enemy—the armor of God, angels, the Chief Shepherd. Help me, Lord, not to be deceived by the deceiver and father of lies. In Jesus' name, amen.

If you . . . know how to give good gifts to your

children, how much more will your Father in

heaven give good gifts to those who ask him!

MATTHEW 7:11

WEEK 16

GIFTS

Maybe we give gifts according to where we are at the time, rather than where the person is who is getting the gift.

Last week, I bought the loveliest handkerchief for my sister. It is old-fashioned looking and has her initial on it. I was in a nostalgic and sentimental mood at the time. My sister is not a very frilly or "fluffy" person, but she will probably like the handkerchief.

This afternoon I bought my friend some "smiley face" pencils for her birthday. I like these pencils, and although the smiley face is not her favorite thing, she will no doubt appreciate the thought behind the gift.

A long time ago, our Father decided to give us a gift. He chose something He wanted to give to us—a bridge back to Him and the relationship He has always wanted to have with us. It cost Him a bundle, but He gave us the gift anyway because He loves us that much.

PRAYER: Lord, thank You that I am Your priceless and treasured possession. Thank You for creating me to fellowship with You, the eternal Jehovah God. Help me, Lord, to understand the depth of that truth. In Jesus' name, amen.

Give thanks to the LORD for He is good;

His love endures forever.

PSALM 107:1

WEEK 17

GOOD TO KNOW

At Thanksgiving...turkey, Pilgrims, Indians and cranberry jelly. Don't forget the pumpkin pie. Thanksgiving—a good time to ask myself, *What am I thankful for?* Even better, *Whom should I thank?*

Parents, a spouse, children, other family members, our home, things, jobs, clothes, food, friends, health—life itself. These are the people and things we want and need in our lives.

Often it seems as if it is a person who deserves our thanks. Sometimes we give the credit to circumstance. Yet ultimately everything we have is a gift from God. Even who we are is a gift from God.

God uses people and situations to channel His gifts to us. He alone is the Great Gift-giver.

It is good to know Whom to thank.

PRAYER: I love You, Lord. Please grant me a grateful heart. In Jesus' name, amen.

Whoever believes in me . . . streams of living

water will flow from within him.

JOHN 7:38

WEEK 18

HEADWATERS

The mighty Roaring Fork River is headquartered in the Colorado Rocky Mountain range along the Continental Divide. The headwaters of that powerful river are deceiving. Up high where the river begins, a narrow, calm stream barely trickles out of the mountain. It meanders and wanders, eventually picking up speed and strength as it continues on its journey.

God promised that rivers of living water would flow out of His believers. He doesn't lie, so the rivers do flow. Right? At the headwaters the stream may be faint, perhaps just a trickle. However, as the water keeps moving, it picks up momentum from and through others—our brothers and sisters—and a mighty, roaring river emerges.

So "keep on keepin' on." You can trust that "The River" will keep on flowing, growing and gaining momentum for the glory of God.

PRAYER: Thank You, Lord, for reminding me in Your Word not to give up meeting with fellow believers. This week, please show me someone to invite to join the believers in worship. In Jesus' name, amen.

Because I live, you also will live.

JOHN 14:19

WEEK 19

HERE AND THERE

One moment we were sitting on a shady porch in wicker rockers with big old shade trees surrounding us, then the next moment we were at a car rental at one of the busiest, most bustling places in the country—the Atlanta airport on a holiday weekend. Here, then there. It was more than a moment, yet it seemed so fast.

Here, and there. With air travel we are here, and shortly after we are there—across the country or even halfway around the world. With computers, we type an electronic note at home or the office, and instantly it reaches its destination.

With banking, our money is in our account; then we wire it someplace, and momentarily it is there. We buy or sell a home, sign an agreement here, and right away we own the home there. Here, and then there, in a moment—a twinkling.

There's a saying, "Two things are certain in life: death and taxes." Life, death; here, there. Now we are here, and then we will be there. The good news is that there is life in death.

Jesus said we could be where He *is*—not *was,* or *will be.* Just before Jesus left this world, He told His friends that He was going away and would prepare a place for us, so we could come there too (John 14:2-3). He also said, "Because I live, you also will live" (John 14:19).

Here, there—that's good news for all who believe in the saving grace of our Lord, Jesus Christ.

PRAYER: Lord, for those of us who are still reeling in shock and grief over the death of a dear loved one, please comfort our hearts. And Lord, please send to me today someone who needs to hear the good news of eternal life through Jesus. Amen.

See, I set before you today life and prosperity,

death and destruction . . . life and death,

blessings and curses. Now choose life,

so that you and your children may live.

DEUTERONOMY 30:15–19

WEEK 20

IMPERCEPTIBLY TURNING

Clearing out clutter and sprucing up after the holidays called for something new from the nearby garden shop. I chose a hardy houseplant and placed the pot outside where it could seen from the kitchen. It looked perfect out there.

One day I glanced out the window and saw the plant all bent over and facing the other way. It had been given plenty of water, so what happened? It had looked so pretty before.

It seemed as though the plant changed direction overnight. Of course it didn't really happen that fast. Actually, it was more like time-lapse photography. Each day the little leaves turned their faces more and more toward the sun. Imperceptibly, the plant was turning ever so slowly. Over a period of time the difference was very noticeable.

Plants don't have a choice; they just do what they do. We, however, do have choices. We can choose what we look at, what we think about and what we absorb.

In our lives, all of the seemingly insignificant decisions we make each day, do matter. As we turn in the direction of our focus, little by little, the choices pile up to create a definite, noticeable change.

The writer of Philippians, Paul, says: "Finally, brothers, whatever is true, whatever is noble, whatever is right, whatever is pure, whatever is lovely, whatever is admirable—if anything is excellent or praiseworthy—think about such things" (Phil. 4:8).

How beautiful we are when we make choices like this—no matter where we are planted!

PRAYER: O God, I think of the saying, "Today is the beginning of the rest of your life." Please help me to make good and wise choices today, and every day. Thank You, Lord! In Jesus' name, amen.

There is a time for everything, and a season

for every activity under heaven.

ECCLESIASTES 3:1

WEEK 21

IN A HURRY

Things can change in a hurry. On Labor Day the leaves of the skinny, white-trunked aspen trees were very green due to a long, wet summer season. Three days later, they were tinged with yellow. In less than a week, the leaves were solid gold. What a majestic sight!

Maybe you, or someone you know, is in a not-so-great place and can't see the light at the end of the tunnel. The situation seems to go on forever, as though it will never change.

Change it will, though. Everything has a season. Nothing is forever, except the love of God. The Bible tells us in the Book of Psalms that the love of the Lord endures forever.

While waiting for our circumstances to change, reading Psalms can give us comfort and assuredness that there is a God who loves us and who does have a good plan for our lives.

Never give up! It's true that it is always darkest just before dawn. Hang in there, and hold on to the Lord. We may get in a rush, but when everything is ready, the situation will change—and probably in a hurry.

PRAYER: Lord, Your ways are not like my ways, and Your timing is not like mine. Please increase my trust in You, Lord; I know that Your timing really is perfect. Thank You, Father. In Jesus' name, amen.

God is our refuge and strength,

an ever-present help in trouble.

PSALM 46:1

WEEK 22

IN THE NIGHT

L ucy is one of my husband's favorite relatives. She is a gentle person, exactly the kind of mother, grandmother, aunt or neighbor you would want to have. Lucy's hair is white and curled and patted down to cover the balding thinness. She walks bent over from the great hump on her back from osteoporosis.

Lucy always has a ready and listening ear. She always has something kind and encouraging to say. You just feel better being around her.

She stays busy with friends and family, but lives alone. Her husband, and best friend of forty-five years, died. I asked her, "How are you really doing?" She paused, then said, "It's hardest in the night. Everything is worse at night."

Lucy's peaceful and pleasant demeanor covers her real feelings of ongoing loneliness and anxiety. In the Book of Samuel, in the Bible, it says that we look at what we can see, but that God looks at the heart.

Sometimes we look "all together" when really we are in our "night." God alone sees into our deepest heart of hearts. He knows what is written there.

He always is about the business of comforting us. He actually provides us with His very presence. That word of hope is really good news—especially in the night.

PRAYER: O God, please reveal Yourself today in a very real way. Comfort my heart, Father, for the secret hurts there. Thank You, Lord. In Jesus' name, amen.

For we were all baptized by

one Spirit into one body.

1 CORINTHIANS 12:13

WEEK 23

IN THE WASH

Have you ever heard the saying, "It'll all come out in the wash"? My mom used to say that phrase. What will come out in the wash, the dirt? the stains? the knots? the tangles? the truth about what it is made of, the quality of the fabric?

It's a good thing—a very good thing—that as children of one heavenly Father, we will come out in the wash all right. The waters of baptism take out all the not-so-good stuff, and the blood of the Savior cleans us up better than ever—forever.

That's good news.

PRAYER: Lord, thank You that though our sins are like scarlet, Your blood washes us white as snow. I praise You, Lord, for Your unending goodness and mercy to me. Hallelujah! Amen.

He is like a tree planted by streams of water,

which yields its fruit in season and whose leaf

does not wither. Whatever he does prospers.

PSALM 1:3

WEEK 24

INSIDE OUT

My husband and I were hiking in the magnificent mountains of Colorado. I was mesmerized by the grandeur and beauty all around. I noticed some huge old pine trees growing out of a big rocky surface. Up toward the tops were pine cones shaped like acorns. I'm no horticulturist, but I know acorns come from oak trees, not pine trees. So I took a closer look.

The small cones had been cone-shaped, but they were now turned nearly inside out. The bottoms were there, but the tops were bare and pointy, like bulbs.

I learned what happens. The cones are shaped as usual when they first appear, but once the seeds inside are dispersed, they look frayed and spent.

Do you ever practice "seed faith"—sowing good seed into good ground—and then feel exhausted and worn out? It is OK to let the Lord "sow seeds" through us, and turn us inside-out. During these times, it's good to remember that we still have our solid base. God *is* our steady, strong tree.

PRAYER: Lord, thank You that You are my rock, my steady and firm foundation. No matter how the winds of adversity might blow, I praise You that I am anchored solidly in You. In Jesus' name, amen.

Be strong and courageous.

Do not be afraid or terrified because of them,

for the LORD *your God goes with you;*

he will never leave you nor forsake you.

DEUTERONOMY 31:6

WEEK 25

IT'S EVERYWHERE!

How beautiful the river was, not massively wide with impressive, grandiose trees along the banks, but simple and wonderful. Here and there were soft little eddies and pools just resting in the water.

The water was clear as a bell and icy cold. From one place on the path I could see that it moved with great speed and strength. Rocks of all sizes—from pebbles to big boulders, smooth and round from the water's continual washing—dotted the river bed and its banks.

The narrow park path wound all over the place—up, down, over the bridge, up again, a sharp left turn, twisting and snaking and then down and to the right. Everywhere I walked, the river was there. It hugged the narrow path; no matter what turns the path took, the river was right there. I thought, *It's everywhere!*

Then I thought of how our lives are so like that path, turning and twisting all over the place. I thought of how the spirit of God is always right there with us, too, throughout our lives—no matter how curvy or straight our path might be.

God has told us, "I will *never* leave you nor forsake you" (Josh. 1:5, emphasis added). Yes, it is true: "The LORD your God will be with you wherever you go" (Josh. 1:9).

Oh, thank, God! That is incredibly comforting—and really good news.

PRAYER: Lord, sometimes I'm "all over the map," so to speak. Thank You that there is no where I can go that You are not already there. In Jesus' name, amen.

Be still, and know that I am God.

PSALM 46:10

WEEK 26

LISTEN TO THE QUIET

When the electricity went out recently, I was impressed with how quiet it was. We live with continual background noise. Indoors we have the sounds of air conditioning units, washers, dryers, televisions, computers, telephones, fax and answering machines, stereos and kids. Outdoors are lawn mowers, leaf blowers, trains, airplanes, insects, birds, dogs, cars and cell phones.

We also have all kinds of noise—thoughts and memories—inside our heads. And what about the noise of our hearts: laughter, crying, murmuring, singing?

I don't think of myself as someone who leads a fast-paced life until I notice how long it takes me to relax and unwind. Getting quiet doesn't happen quickly for me. Sometimes I even have to work consciously at it. But even David, songwriter extraordinaire, wise warrior and anointed King of Israel, needed to be reminded by God to "Be still, and know that I am God" (Ps. 46:10).

It's a noisy world, and we all need a quiet place in the midst of the noise—a safe place where we can be still and hear the Lord. Ask Him to help you find that safe, quiet place. Then, go there and see what wonderful surprises Jesus has planned to share with you.

PRAYER: Thank You, Father, that I can come to You anytime, that I can pray and be in communication with You. Lord, thank You for the peace and direction I get from simply being in Your presence. In Jesus' name, amen.

Thanks be to God, who always leads us

in triumphal procession in Christ

and through us spreads everywhere

the fragrance of the knowledge of him.

2 CORINTHIANS 2:14

WEEK 27

LONG AFTER

My mom's favorite flower was the gardenia. When I was young, I remember her wearing one in her hair on festive occasions. Mom is no longer here, but my dad maintains a beautiful gardenia bush in his yard in her memory.

Gardenias are the most potent smelling flower I know; the pungent fragrance of just one flower can fill an entire room. But, the blooms don't last very long. The smooth, ivory petals turn yellow, then brown, and too quickly they look dried up and ugly.

Funny thing about gardenias: long after the appearance of the flower starts to go downhill, the powerfully sweet odor is every bit as strong as it ever was.

Interesting thing about saints: long after our outward appearance begins to degenerate due to aging, accidents or disease, we still radiate a glorious aroma to the world. The spirit in our hearts never dies or disintegrates.

And you can bet that when one of us leaves this world, there remains a sweet smelling fragrance—long after.

PRAYER: Father, I praise and thank You for filling me with Your glorious Holy Spirit. Thank You that Holy Spirit is a lovely fragrance that will attract others to You. In Jesus' name, amen.

God is our refuge and strength,

an ever-present help in trouble.

PSALM 46:1

WEEK 28

NEARLY DEADLY

She was from another country. She tried hard to communicate and fit in. She read books to learn the language. She watched television to study the vernacular. She was a cheerful, pleasant person. She hired out to different families as a pediatric nurse taking care of babies. There were long nights and long weeks away from her new husband, home, family, friends and anything familiar. She had put all of her trust and hope in the fellow who married her and brought her to this country. She leaned hard on him, looked to him for her every need.

Things seemed as if they were going pretty well. Then unexpectedly they found her, nearly dead from an attempted suicide. Drugs and alcohol were listed as the cause. But what really nearly killed her was disillusionment. Her trust and hope had been crushed. She had made her husband the "everything" in her life. When he took up with a younger woman, she could not cope.

People are just people—not perfect and not God. Sooner or later people say or do things that do not meet our expectations and that disappoint us. There is only One who will never fail us or disappoint us. Jesus *is* and *always will be* there to trust and lean on. We can always count on Him. That's good news.

PRAYER: Thank You, Lord, that I can count on You, all the time. No matter what life throws my way, You are there for me, to walk me through it and to comfort me. Amen.

He has made everything beautiful in its time.

ECCLESIASTES 3:11

WEEK 29

NEW GROWTH

I t is springtime, and even here in South Florida there are signs of new growth all about. This morning while walking, I noticed all the light coloring of the season. The grass and all the varied trees are in their glorious pastel shades of green. It is so pretty, yet not nearly as eye-catching and dramatic as the darker, more vibrant colors of mature growth in full bloom.

Similarly, in our Christian walk, we are more pale and stand out less in the earlier parts of our journey. As we grow and mature and "hang out" with Jesus, we take on deeper, richer, more brilliant hues of the attributes of Jesus Himself. We are easier to spot, singled out more quickly.

God grows us all beautiful in His time. That's good news.

PRAYER: Thank You, Lord, that I am a new creation in Christ, that the old is gone and the new is here. Thank You for growing me into the likeness of Christ, from glory to glory. In Jesus' name, amen.

With the Lord a day is like a thousand years,

and a thousand years are like a day.

2 PETER 3:8

WEEK 30

NO CONCEPT OF TIME

She definitely was a member of our family—Bailey, a beautiful twelve-year-old buff cocker spaniel. Over the years, we had had a lot of fun with Bailey. When she was a puppy we would go in and out of the house and watch how excited she would get every time we came back in. Each time she would go bonkers because she was so glad to see us. Her tail would just about wag off.

Bailey had no concept of time. If we were gone for hours, days or just moments, she didn't know the difference. All she knew was that we were gone and then we were there.

Our eight young grandchildren have no concept of time yet. They are always so happy to see us. It doesn't matter how much time has elapsed since seeing them last, they are always just so glad to see us whenever they do.

Adults do have a concept of time. And yet, time is a weird thing for us. The older we get, the more we wonder where it has gone.

God has an even different concept of time. Yet each time He gazes on us, He is thrilled beyond measure. We are His creations, the works of His hands, and He loves us beyond anything we can comprehend. We sometimes mess up and we are far from perfect, but He is crazy about us—just the way we are!

That is good news.

PRAYER: Thank You, Lord, that You love me, and that no matter what, you will still love me. In Jesus' name, amen.

I will not forget you! See, I have engraved you

on the palms of my hands.

ISAIAH 49:15–16

Week 31

No Name Tags

It was Saturday morning, and I decided to try and beat the crowd to the grocery store. I was in line to pay, and overheard a customer telling the cashier that she had just come back from a trip to her class reunion. She bubbled, explaining how much fun it was to see people from "'way back then." As she continued on about how much everyone had changed, she said, "In fact, it's a good thing we had name tags or we might not have known each other!"

Time does have a way of doing that. Isn't it good to know that there is someone who will always know us—even without name tags—no matter how life or aging may have changed our appearance?

We are told in Jeremiah 1:5 that our wonderful heavenly Father has known us since before way back when. He always recognizes us. And, He is filled with delight every time He looks at us! That's good news.

PRAYER: Thank You, Lord, that You always have my name written on the palm of Your hand. Thank You that I am continually on Your mind, and that You will never ever forget me. In Jesus' name, amen.

Everyone who calls on

the name of the LORD will be saved.

JOEL 2:32; ACTS 2:21;

ROMANS 10:13

WEEK 32

NO TIME

As a child, I was only concerned with what was going on "right now"—living fully in the moment with no cares about anything else. Certainly I never gave a thought to dying, even though we all die sooner or later.

For the victims of the recent dreadful terrorist disasters, it was sooner, and not later. For them, there was no time. No time to take care of unfinished business. No time to say or do something they had planned to do someday (the "Isle of Later"). No time to think about the hereafter—where they would be going, forever.

It is so easy to procrastinate and put things off, especially important decisions. I have the best intentions, yet getting "a round tuit" often gets left in the dust for immediate priorities.

But the most important decision we could ever make is one we don't have to put off, not for a single second. It isn't something we can get someone else to do for us, nor is it a lengthy, time-consuming task. It is simple: Several Bible passages say that if we seek the Lord honestly, with our hearts, and call on Him, we will be found by Him, and saved. Not just a few, not only the called and chosen, but everyone. It is also said that if we forsake Him, He will reject us forever.

Today, while we have time, let's be sure that we have taken that step to seek the Lord, to call on His name, and be found by Him. He is just waiting for that—with open arms and a loving heart.

PRAYER: Thank You, Lord, that You are my ultimate loving Father, that You are always turned toward me, seeking me out and wanting me to come home to You. In Jesus' name, amen.

In addition to all this, take up the shield

of faith, with which you can extinguish all the

flaming arrows of the evil one.

EPHESIANS 6:16

WEEK 33

OPEN SEASON

This morning at breakfast my husband quipped, "Today is a good day not to be a lobster!" True; it is minilobster time—two days for the public to catch lobsters before the commercial season opens.

Here in the sparkling turquoise waters, year-around open season for lobster is out of the question. These shellfish take many years to reach a size legal to catch. Were the diving rules not regulated, the sea would be raped, pillaged and stripped of these delicacies.

We, however, are in open season at all times. In 1 Peter 5:8 we are told that our adversary prowls about like a lion in order to devour us. And Satan doesn't just lie around, waiting for us to make a move. No, he is "on the prowl," and it isn't merely to thwart our plans, upset or discourage us. He comes to "rob, kill and destroy." He is a very real and very dangerous enemy!

The Psalms are filled with affirmations of the Lord's protection. In his high priestly prayer just before he was crucified, Jesus talks to His Father about us, "My prayer is not that you take them out of the world but that you protect them from the evil one" (John 17:15). And the same Paul who warned us about that "lion" says in his letter to the people at Thessalonica, "But the Lord is faithful, and he will strengthen and protect you from the evil one" (2 Thess. 3:3).

Praise be to our Lord God who daily strengthens us and preserves us from all harm and danger!

PRAYER: Lord, I know I'm in a war today and every day. Thanks be to You, O God, who can protect me from the evil one. I pray the blood of Jesus over me, and ask for You to dispatch angels to protect me this day and night. Thank You, Lord. In Jesus' name, amen.

He who began a good work in you

will carry it on to completion.

PHILIPPIANS 1:6

WEEK 34

PLAYING SCHOOL

Last week we got together for a family dinner. I had tried to think of what the younger ones might like to eat, but when they arrived, the kids could not have cared less about dinner. They would rather play than eat. They had a great time getting dirty and making Grandma nervous as they ran around the edge of the water.

Everyone came inside at dinnertime. The kids went to the back room where the dress-up box lives, which provided a rare opportunity for just the adults to catch up. We did have a few surprise visits, though, as the children paraded in their favorite costumes.

Later in the evening, a wave of memories rolled over me, and I thought of how as kids our whole lives had been about playing. It took all our time and a lot of energy. It wore us out. And, it readied us for adult life and the real world.

I couldn't help but think, *Now I'm grown and I still like to play!* There's one kind of playing that takes a lot of planning, effort and time on my part, yet doesn't prepare me for anything except frustration and disappointment. That is "playing God." Life is uphill for me when I fall into the trap of playing God.

A Bible verse says we can grow up in the Lord (1 Pet. 2:2). Twelve step programs teach us to let God be God. Here is a little letter that I keep on my desk as a daily reminder:

> Good morning, I will be handling all your problems today. I will not need your help . . . so have a great day! God.

PRAYER: Thank You, Lord, that I don't have to be God today, that I can still just play but not wear the "Jr. God badge." In Jesus' name, amen.

Everyone who asks receives; he who seeks finds;

and to him who knocks, the door will be opened.

LUKE 11:10

WEEK 35

POLLS

Many kinds of polls exist. Some surveys are honest, some not so honest. A few are designed by companies to prove or justify a product or a person. Some may be helpful in advertising and ultimately in sales.

A friend of mine polls his acquaintances when he's looking for people to agree with his point of view, rather than seeking out those who have a different perspective from his.

There are times when I pray for God's advice or direction. Sometimes what I am really doing is looking for confirmation—an approval to go ahead with my own ideas and plans.

If I am going to ask the Almighty God of the Universe for His opinion, perhaps I would be wise to keep an open mind to receive His answers.

PRAYER: Your ways are not like my ways, Lord, and Your thoughts not like mine. Do I trust You, God, when I pray? when I come to You for direction and wisdom? God, grant me an increase in faith and trust. In Jesus' name, amen.

Come to me, all you who are weary and

burdened, and I will give you rest.

MATTHEW 11:28

WEEK 36

POOLS

L ast night it rained. Lots of rain. Lots of thunder and lightning. This morning the river seemed to be hustling along more rapidly than yesterday.

From our balcony I spied a small pool and kept watching it for fish. The guide who accompanied us on our first fly-fishing adventure said to look for trout in the pools of the river. Sure enough, when the sun was fully out—shining down—I could see a beautiful rainbow trout. He was so still I'd have thought he was dead if he had not been upright in the water.

In the quieter spots of our lives—the pools—where there is not a lot of motion, there is still something going on. There may not be the hustle-bustle rush and turmoil of everyday life, yet all around is a bubbling, effervescent world whose waters flow around us continually.

There is life there, in the resting—life and renewal and refreshing. When it is time, we'll move out of the pool and into the current, back into the rapid flow of the river.

In the Book of Psalms it says, "Be still, and know that I am God" (Ps. 46:10). Thank God for the pools He provides for us in our lives.

PRAYER: Lord, I am so busy in my life. Help me to make wise choices and to spend time being still, with You. In Jesus' name, amen.

I baptize you with water for repentance.

But after me . . . He will baptize you with

the Holy Spirit and with fire.

MATTHEW 3:11

WEEK 37

RAGING

This has been a hot, dry summer. Forest fires are out of control in many counties of our state. People have been forced to leave their homes, businesses and houses. Beautiful trees and wildlife sanctuaries are threatened. Could there be anything at all good about the raging fires?

Do fires ever rage in my life? Do I start them myself, or are they the work of an arsonist?

As for the bad, it's obvious—it is destruction.

As for the good, well, a little out-of-control burning by the Holy Spirit could be a wonderful thing.

Something to think about . . .

PRAYER: Lord, light a fire in me today. Let it burn off the "yucky stuff" in my life, and let what is left glow brightly that it might attract people to Jesus. Thank You, Lord! Amen.

Therefore, if anyone is in Christ, he is a new

creation; the old has gone, the new has come!

2 CORINTHIANS 5:17

WEEK 38

RAGS AT THE BANQUET

Once upon a time a man—clad only in the dirtiest of rags—lived in the streets. One day a person from the palace approached him. There was going to be a banquet at the palace, and people from the highways and byways were being invited. "Would he like to come?"

The man was indeed interested, however, he could not attend dressed in rags. The palace representative assured him that his rags would be exchanged for some suitable finery.

All was in order. The men arrived at the palace and went directly to the King's dressing chambers. Servants bundled the filthy rags and scrubbed the man clean. He was then allowed to choose robes from the King's closets. Whatever he chose he could keep, so the man carefully examined the many garments and garbed himself in the finest silk and satin. He was ready for the banquet!

As they left the dressing quarters, the man grabbed his old rags. He insisted on taking the filthy bundle; he felt more secure holding on to it. The man, resplendent in his fine attire, joined the banquet and yet still clung to the dirty bundle. So distracted by clinging to his bag, the man never ate and he left the banquet hungry.

The evening ended. Everyone was stuffed—everyone except the man clinging to his rag bundle.

Today Jesus invites all of us to God's great banquet—to leave our old ways and old rags, and to say "Yes!" to Him and to a new and glorious way of living. That is good news!

PRAYER: Lord, Your Word says that I am a new creation in Christ. Help me not to stay with the ways of my old self, but to walk in newness of life with You today. Thank You, Lord. Amen.

Even the Son of Man did not come to be served,

but to serve, and to give his life

as a ransom for many.

MARK 10:45

WEEK 39

RED, BLUE, PURPLE

Our hands and feet have more little-bitty bones than any other part of our whole body. Nerve endings—for pain sensitivity—are closer to the surface in our hands than anywhere else on our bodies. When I get my finger stuck for a blood test it only hurts a little, for a second, but I dread it.

So when the soldiers wanted to kill Jesus, they pounded nails into His hands and feet—the very worst places for pain. Long, rough, square spikes are what served as nails then. I do not know how He didn't pass out instantly with the very first wound. It wasn't only death, but also the worst torture.

No one can live without blood. When your blood goes out of your body, you die. Without blood, there is death, not life.

The blood in Jesus' veins might have looked blue. It was "true blue"; He Himself is actual "Truth" in the body of a man. The blood in Jesus came out of His hands and feet all red and gushy. His blood was as red as yours or mine.

Jesus' blood was red and blue. Red and blue—purple. Purple represents royalty. Jesus is the King of Kings, the Lord of Lords!

When you look at your skin, the veins may look bluish. They are—truly. Inside your veins, the blood is red, through Communion, we get a "blood transfusion." Red, blue—purple. We're royalty, children of the King: red, blue—purple.

Life is in the blood—above all, in the blood of Jesus. That, is *good* news.

PRAYER: Father, I cannot live forever without the atoning blood of Jesus. Thank You for this sacrifice. I can never thank You enough; please help me simply receive Your glorious gift of grace. Thank You, Lord. Amen.

So then, just as you received Christ Jesus as

Lord, continue to live in him, rooted and built

up in him, strengthened in the faith as you were

taught, and overflowing with thankfulness.

COLOSSIANS 2:6–7

WEEK 40

ROOTS

The roots on our elephant ear philodendron or "eyeball tree," as my precious five-year-old granddaughter, Taylor, calls it, keep shooting out. They are strong and fibrous, thin and flexible. When they get long enough to reach down into the decking, I wrap them around the trunk to prevent their rooting in the earth under the wood deck.

Aren't we like those roots, springing up and reaching out, waving in the breeze, always turning toward the sun? Isn't God always there, gently turning us downward so our roots can be firmly and deeply in Him? He is continuously and gently doing this, even though it is barely noticeable to us.

It *is* necessary, though, in order to steady the large, heavy top growth of the plant—the visible part. Then when the storms come, we will not topple, but stand firm, rooted deeply in Him.

Thank You, Lord, for faithfully taking care of rooting us, even though we are not aware of it.

PRAYER: Father, help me not to get top-heavy by doing things that we can just see. Help me to grow deep, sturdy roots in You through communion in prayer with You each day. Thank You, Father. In Jesus' name, amen.

For the word of God is living and active.

Sharper than any double-edged sword, it

penetrates even to dividing soul and spirit,

joints and marrow; it judges the thoughts

and attitudes of the heart.

HEBREWS 4:12

WEEK 41

ROUNDS

I n our back yard we have two bird feeders. Since I try to attract cardinals, I keep them filled with sunflower seeds. Early in the mornings, or late in the afternoons, the birds make their rounds. Seems as if they spend all their time looking for food. From one feeder to another, they continually hunt for something to eat.

On the other hand, my dog will eat anything—well, anything except dill pickles. And she doesn't much like olives either. But she will eat anything else. Lettuce. Tomatoes. She'll even lick a lemon. She isn't picky about what she eats or how much she eats.

We sometimes make the rounds looking for spiritual "food." We go from place to place—from New Age literature to Zen—trying to find something that will satisfy us.

But nothing seems to, except the Bible. We don't have to settle for just anything in our searching for spiritual nourishment. The Word of God is right in front of us all the time.

There is a saying, "Don't read just any book, read the best." Spiritually speaking, we have a smorgasbord of the best food available to us in the Bible. We can literally feast to our heart is content, and be glad we did!

Do I make use of the very best "food" there is? Not nearly enough. Thank God we have it! And I resolve, again, to go there first—before I make the rounds.

PRAYER: Lord, it is no accident that the Bible is the best-selling book of all time. It holds the road map for the journey of my life. Holy Spirit, inspire me to read Your word, which is so alive this very day. In Jesus' name, amen.

The LORD is close to the brokenhearted

and saves those who are crushed in spirit.

PSALM 34:18

WEEK 42

SOMETHING YOU NEVER HAD

Cindy waited thirty-four long years and stayed in the marriage. She gave it her all, and waited for her husband to come around. He was emotionally unavailable. He dropped dead from a heart attack last month. Bye-bye to that hope. Sam is fifty-eight years old. There has been a hole in his heart as big as all outdoors for fifty-six of those years, wanting his father who disappeared when Sam was two. Dianne has been looking for someone to come into her life for many years—a partner and lover. She is old now. It may not happen.

Have you ever longed for something you've never had? something money can't buy? maybe a good relationship with your mother or father, or your kids? Perhaps you would really like a relationship that is now impossible because that person has died?

You can be sad about something you never had. You can grieve for something you never will have. But can you lose something you have never had?

One thing you can never lose—even if you want to—is the unconditional love that God your Father has for you. Never. No way! Not possible to lose that; it's there forever and ever. It's just for you.

The *love* that *God* has for *you* is not—and never could be—something you never had. It's been there for all of your life. Even before. And it will be after.

Just ask him to show you. He will!

PRAYER: O God, sometimes only You know the pain and anguish that I have. Thank You for caring about me. Please come today and comfort me and heal my broken heart, as You promise. Thank You, Father, in Jesus' name, amen.

You will be a crown of splendor in the LORD'S

hand, a royal diadem in the hand of your God.

ISAIAH 62:3

WEEK 43

SPARKLE AND SHIMMER

Those skinny white-trunked trees related to the birches are aspens. They are so beautiful. In the summer the heart shaped leaves are a lustrous green on top; the underside is a flat, grayish green. As the breeze flutters through, the leaves sparkle and shimmer like no other tree. It is so eye-catching!

In autumn, the leaves turn a glorious gold, and when those small trees are massed together over all the face of a mountain, it is breathtaking.

Individually, we are—each one of us—beautiful, too. We are jewels, created by God—precious, priceless and irreplaceable. When the breeze of God's Holy Spirit blows on us and through us, we sparkle and shimmer. It, too, is so eye-catching! Sparkling and shimmering, what a great way to effortlessly shine—and share—the love and beauty of God!

If you do not have a personal relationship with Him, seek Him today. Ask Him to send His Spirit through you, like the breeze through the aspens. He will.

PRAYER: Lord, please come into my life anew today. Come, Holy Spirit, breathe newness of life into me. Thank You, Lord! In Jesus' name, amen.

This is what the LORD says—he who

created you . . . he who formed you . . .

Fear not, for I have redeemed you;

I have summoned you by name; you are mine.

ISAIAH 43:1

WEEK 44

STAND OUT ROSE

O n the side of our house, my husband has a rose garden. He plants, prunes, fertilizes and sprays the small
bushes. We so enjoy the beauty of the blooms, as well
as their wonderful fragrance.

A few months ago, he set aside two or three of the rose bushes
still in plastic pots. They were nearly dead and he planned to throw
them away, but he forgot. So the bushes stayed there, and they
became overgrown with tall grass and weeds.

When I opened the mini-blinds, I immediately noticed this tiny
rosebud outside of the window. The bud stood out because of the
bright color contrasting the dark shades of green all around it. The
stem was about a foot high, and the little flower was a beautiful
pinkish-orange hue.

There it was, rising out of the midst of the stubble and weeds.
It's amazing what God can grow out of an overgrown cast-off pot.
He is the One who can grow something beautiful *out* of anything,
and *in* everyone. In fact, He is just waiting for the chance for us to
let Him.

That's good news!

*PRAYER: Father, I praise You and thank You that You love me as
I am, yet see me as I will be. Thank You that You are continually about
the business of making something beautiful of me. In Jesus' name, amen.*

Peace I leave with you; my peace I give to you.

I do not give to you as the world gives.

Do not let your hearts be troubled

and do not be afraid.

JOHN 14:27

WEEK 45

"SUMMER-TARY"

All five of us took the flowers and helped arrange them in the urn at the cemetery. A day's outing at Grandma's for Benjamin, McCallen, Courtney and Taylor included a stop at Great Pop's and a stop at the grave site of Meem. We had silk pink lilies for Easter. The kids found some castoff white glads, with which we padded the lilies into the urn.

The kids instinctively reverenced the place. I know this because they didn't run around like they usually do. When leaving, Courtney called out the window in her wonderful big voice, "Goodbye, all you 'Summer-tary' people!"

"Summer-tary." Not solitary. And not the season of winter with which we usually associate death. Summer—the full, peak bloom of life. Out of the mouths of babes . . .

PRAYER: Father, thank You that You have provided a way for me to be with You eternally—the "summer" of forever. Thank You, Jesus, for Your shed blood so that I might be reconciled with You. Thank You that the sting of death is gone. In Jesus' mighty name, amen.

I have set my rainbow in the clouds,

and it will be the sign of the

covenant between me and the earth.

GENESIS 9:13

WEEK 46

TALKING RAINBOWS

A friend and I were on our way to a meeting. The morning was dismally gray, and rush hour traffic was bumper-to-bumper. My friend was despondent. She shared with me how it seemed that her life was falling apart around her, even as she kept living it. I was listening, yet in my mind I was trying to formulate words of encouragement for her.

Then we saw it! Right there in front of us—double rainbows—huge, stretching all the way from far left to far right in the sky, one directly over the other. What a sight! Not just one rainbow, but a double rainbow with a double message of the gift of comfort and hope that God gives us because of His presence and His word.

Rainbows are the colors of God's love. Nonscientifically speaking, He is light, and His light is refracted and beautifully reflected through moisture into a visible arc of red, orange, yellow, green, blue and violet.

Rainbows speak of a promise God gave a long time ago. After the flood that destroyed nearly all life, God made a covenant with Noah and his descendants for all generations to come—never again would He destroy the earth by water. The rainbow is the sign of the covenant.

Do rainbows talk to us today? You bet they do. They did the talking for me the day my friend needed a good word! Each time we see one—or two!—we can be reminded of the faithfulness of God toward us. That is good news.

PRAYER: Lord, thank You for the visible signs You show me to help me recall Your Word and Your faithfulness. I praise You, Lord, for Your unending glory and goodness. Amen.

You are precious and honored in my sight,

and . . . I love you.

ISAIAH 43:4

WEEK 47

THE CANDY SHELVES

She was maybe five or six years old. She was waiting for her mom there in the drugstore, and she was standing near the cash register, her eyes glued to the candy shelves. For that little girl, paradise was just a few feet and a few dimes away.

Different times, different things. When we are babies we want our bottle. In grade school we want only to be with our friends. Teenagers want romance—and a car! Then we want a job, a home, a family. And a fulfilling life. Happiness. Security in a changing world. Retirement investments. Good health.

Throughout all our ages and stages we want a *lot* of different things. But God always wants the same thing—us.

In the Bible, God tells us that He created us for fellowship with Him, and He relentlessly pursues us and that relationship. We are restless in our spirits until we are "with Him."

He won't give up, and He won't give in. He will continue to lovingly gaze upon you as if you, yourself, are those candy shelves.

PRAYER: Thank You, Lord, that You never give up on me, and that You always seek me out. Thank You for Your unending love for me. Amen.

He calls his own sheep by name and

leads them out . . . he goes on ahead of them,

and his sheep follow him because

they know his voice.

JOHN 10:3-4

WEEK 48

THE VOICE

We were sitting around rehashing ball games, slumber parties, teachers and who went steady with whom. Yep, we were getting ready for another class reunion. How do they come around so often? Every ten or twenty years; doesn't seem like they ought to crop up so "often!"

The last reunion, I remember thinking that the guys had definitely changed more than the girls had, especially in the hair department! I recall looking at the yearbook picture name tags; how memories came flooding back.

One thing from that reunion stands out most in my mind. Although most of our appearances were drastically different from high school days, one thing had not changed one iota; that was our voices. I discovered I could identify people when I heard them speak, even if I didn't recognize them from the way they looked.

How interesting. I thought of what Jesus said: the sheep listen to the shepherd's voice, and they follow him because they know his voice. They will never follow a stranger because they don't recognize his voice.

How great to think that as we listen to the voice of our own Shepherd, Jesus, and follow Him, we won't get misled or go off in the wrong direction.

He is speaking, and we know His voice. It is love, and it never changes. That is good news.

PRAYER: Father, thank You that Your voice is love. Thank You for allowing me to recognize it, at all times and in all circumstances, especially as You speak to my heart. In Jesus' name, amen.

He heals the brokenhearted and

binds up their wounds.

PSALM 147:3

WEEK 49

VERTICAL BEFORE HORIZONTAL

Recently something that was emotionally traumatic for me happened in our family. It knocked me down; it felt as if I had been slugged. I got up though. Soon after, there was another emotionally charged event. I felt whacked around again, and this time I had to struggle to get up. On the heels of this was a third occurrence. This time I tried to get up, but couldn't.

The Good Shepherd came looking for me. I wasn't lost, but I was beaten up and bruised. Nonetheless, He came to where I was. He picked me up, and instead of slinging me over His shoulder and taking me home, He carried me in His arms. He stroked my hair. He soothed my forehead. He rubbed my feet. He fed me by hand. And when I became tired, He held me right there in His arms while I slept.

Before long my legs got strong again. What a perfectly wonderful Shepherd! I felt renewed and refreshed. Then He set me down to romp with the other lambs and sheep again.

This is why the vertical has to come before the horizontal. Our relationship with Him must precede all else.

PRAYER: Father, thank You that You are always in the restoration business. Thank You for seeking me out when I am lost and hurting and thank You for healing me. In Jesus' name, amen.

You are the light of the world.

A city on a hill cannot be hidden.

MATTHEW 5:14

WEEK 50

WALKING IN WHITE

W hile worshipping recently at a nearby church, we sang a song that asked God to send His fire so we could walk in white in the world today. I thought to myself, *I don't know if I can sing that, honestly. We have just seen fire destroy giant buildings and kill countless numbers of people in New York City and Washington, D.C., and I don't know if I want fire sent to me!*

I seemed to hear an answer to my unspoken thoughts: "The fire of the world destroys, but the fire of the Spirit cleans up and purifies." *OK,* I thought, *I can sing that.*

Then, in my mind's eye, I saw a garden. Jesus was there, clothed in white. I walked up to Him and said, "O! You look so beautiful in that white robe!" He told me He had a white robe for me. I replied, "Yes, I know, when I die I'll get a white robe." "No, now!" He said.

Yes, we need those white robes now, not after we're dead so we can wear them like a badge. We need power today to walk in white and be a light in this dark and scary world.

And when we are just going about our everyday business, if we can try to remember that we are wearing beautiful white robes that Jesus gave to us, perhaps it will help us to share Him more boldly with everyone we encounter.

PRAYER: Thank You, Lord, for the opportunity and privilege to share Jesus. Help me today to keep my light burning brightly so those around me, still in darkness, can see Your great love and Your caring. Amen.

My word . . . will not return to me empty,

but will accomplish what I desire

and achieve the purpose for which I sent it.

ISAIAH 55:11

WEEK 51

WHERE DOES IT GO?

L ast summer we saw heavy rains and a lot of flooding across the country. Where does all that water go? When there's a flash flood, or a super heavy rain, where does *all* of that water go? Some evaporates into the atmosphere and creates moisture in the air we—along with plants and animals—need to breathe. Most runs off and seeps into the earth.

When we flood ourselves with the Word of God, when we soak and saturate our minds and hearts with thoughts and messages from the Lord, it is the same. Some of it evaporates into the sphere of our relationships; other people absorb and breathe it in, and it nourishes them. Most of it works its way deep down into our spirits to give drink to our spiritual roots and to sustain us in dry times.

Isaiah 55:10-11 says, "As the rain and the snow come down from heaven, and do not return to it without watering the earth and making it bud and flourish, so that it yields seed for the sower and bread for the eater, so is my word that goes out from my mouth: it will not return to me empty, but will accomplish what I desire and achieve the purpose for which I sent it."

Thank You, Lord, that the water goes somewhere!

PRAYER: Father, what a great gift Your Word is. Thank You that I can see it, read it, and listen to it anytime. Help me to earnestly desire the wisdom of Your Word today, Father, as I grow from glory to glory in You. In Jesus' name, amen.

Trust in the LORD with all your heart,

and lean not on your own understanding;

in all your ways acknowledge Him

and will make your paths straight.

PROVERBS 3:5–6

WEEK 52

WHITE BUTTERFLY

My husband and I were threading our way down the path from our trek up to the waterfall. Nothing around. No people, no birds, no animals—except for one very small chipmunk scurrying from rock to rock to avoid our big scary shoes coming toward him.

Then a tiny white butterfly appeared. It fluttered along in front of us, as if leading the way. All the way down the trail to the bridge at the bottom, there by the river's edge, it flew into the woods, only to reappear behind us when we moved on.

We were not lost. But sometimes we don't have to be completely lost to need a little guidance and direction or even reassurance.

Ten thousand feet up in the Rocky Mountains, a little white butterfly became a reminder saying that God goes ahead of us to lead the way and also comes behind us.

God tells us in the Bible, "I will never leave you or forsake you" (Josh. 1; Deut. 31; Heb. 13).

It's a promise! That's good news.

PRAYER: Thank You, Father, that You send your Holy Spirit to guide me, to go before me, and to be my helper and my comforter, no matter where I am. Amen

INDEX